Real-Life Superpowers

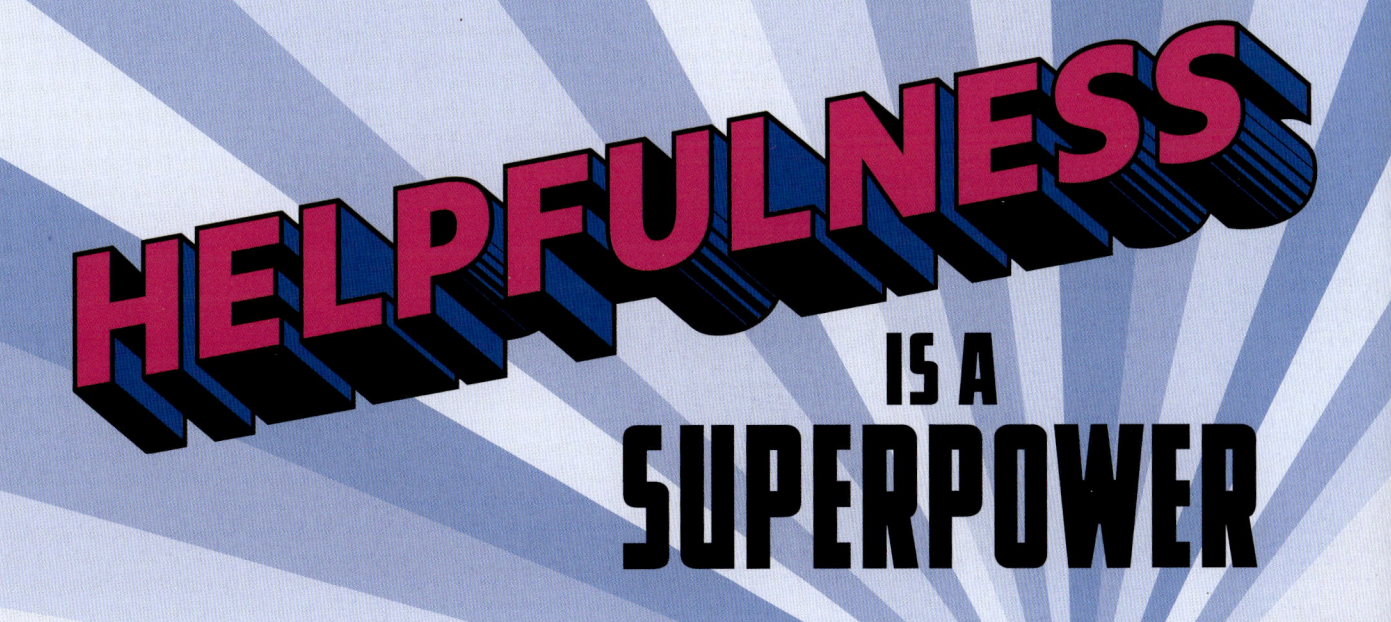

HELPFULNESS IS A SUPERPOWER

by Mari Schuh

PEBBLE
a capstone imprint

Published by Pebble, an imprint of Capstone
1710 Roe Crest Drive, North Mankato, Minnesota 56003
capstonepub.com

Copyright © 2024 by Capstone. All rights reserved. No part of this publication may be reproduced in whole or in part, or stored in a retrieval system, or transmitted in any form or by any means, electronic, mechanical, photocopying, recording, or otherwise, without written permission of the publisher.

Library of Congress Cataloging-in-Publication Data is available on the Library of Congress website.

ISBN: 9780756576769 (hardcover)
ISBN: 9780756576714 (paperback)
ISBN: 9780756576721 (ebook PDF)

Summary: You do your chores without being asked. You help a classmate with their homework. You volunteer to help those in your community. When you're helpful, you can make someone's day better! Learn more about this real-life superpower and how you can use it in your life.

Image Credits
Getty Images: Caia Image, 6, FG Trade, 8, iStock/Chris Ryan, 4, kate_sept2004, 11, Kevin Dodge, 12, Klaus Vedfelt, 17, Maskot, 16, Milko, 18, Moyo Studio, Cover, Nick David, 10, SDI Productions, 9, skynesher, 15, SolStock, 7, Thomas Barwick, 5; Shutterstock: Kapitosh, design element (background), Matt Benoit, 20 (bottom right),Monkey Business Images, 14, 19, patpitchaya, 20 (bottom middle), Prostock-studio, 13

Editorial Credits
Editor: Alison Deering; Designer: Bobbie Nuytten; Media Researcher: Rebekah Hubstenberger; Production Specialist: Whitney Schaefer

All internet sites appearing in back matter were available and accurate when this book was sent to press.

Printed and bound in China. PO 5593

Table of Contents

Helping Matters 4

Helping at Home 10

Helping at School 14

Helping Yourself 18

    Calendar of Helpfulness 20

    Glossary 22

    Read More 23

    Internet Sites 23

    Index 24

    About the Author 24

Words in **bold** are in the glossary.

Helping Matters

Did you help someone today? What did you do? Maybe you helped a teammate who fell. Or maybe you helped set the table for dinner.

People who are helpful make things easier for others. They put other people first. They help without being asked. Helpful people do not expect anything in return.

Helpfulness is a **superpower**. People who are helpful care about others. They are kind and thoughtful. Being helpful can also build **confidence**. It reminds us that we belong to a **community**.

Helping people feels good. You help your friends and family. You might also help people you don't know well. Being helpful usually does not take a lot of time. It often does not cost any money either.

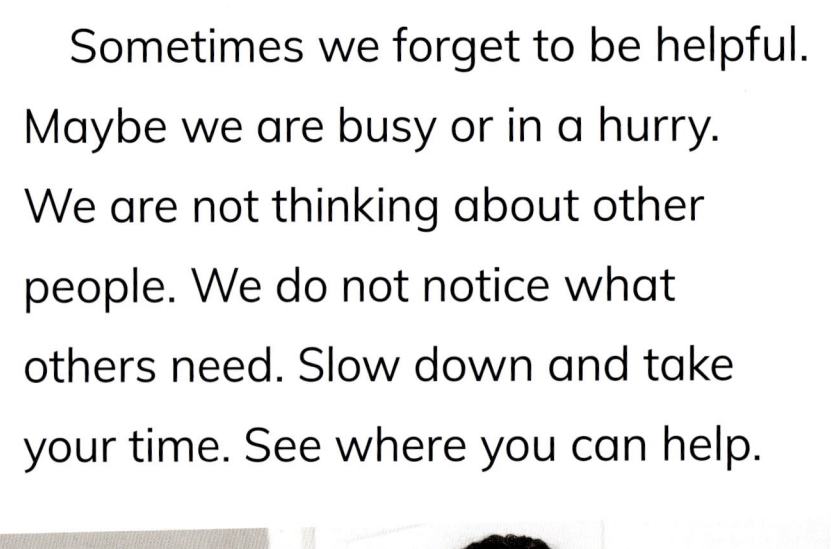

Sometimes we forget to be helpful. Maybe we are busy or in a hurry. We are not thinking about other people. We do not notice what others need. Slow down and take your time. See where you can help.

Ahmed thinks about people who have less than him. He **donates** clothes and toys. Becky cares about people in need. She **volunteers** at a shelter. She helps serve food to hungry families.

Helping at Home

You can be helpful at home every day. Look around your home to see how you can help. Vacuum the living room. Dust the furniture, and water the plants.

Do **chores** without being asked. Make your bed in the morning. Help your parents rake leaves. You are helping your family!

Kia is helpful at home. She brushes her cat's fur to keep it healthy. She helps her grandpa put on a sweater. When her brother's baseball team loses a game, Kia listens. She helps him feel better.

Jonah is a helpful brother. When his sister is sick, he brings her medicine and a glass of water. He plays quietly so his sister can rest. Jonah also does his sister's chores for her.

Helping at School

Being helpful makes you a good friend. Is a classmate having a bad day? Be thoughtful and kind. Sit with them at lunch. Play with them at recess. This could help them feel better.

Sharing your things also shows you are helpful. Kevin forgot his notebook. Sasha wants to help. She gives Kevin some paper from her notebook. Now they can both do their schoolwork.

Paulo cares about his school. He helps to keep it clean. When he sees **litter** in the hallway, he puts it in a trash can. He **recycles** cans and boxes. At lunch, he does not leave the table messy. He makes sure it is clean.

Nova is also helpful at school. She listens to and **respects** her teacher. She raises her hand before answering a question. This helps her teacher lead the lesson.

Helping Yourself

How can you help yourself? Start by taking care of yourself. Stay active and eat healthy foods. Take breaks when you are tired. Get enough sleep. If you are stressed, talk to an adult you trust. Tell them how you feel.

Taking good care of yourself makes you feel healthy and strong. When you feel good, it's easier to help others. It's fun to use your superpowers!

Calendar of Helpfulness

Helping others is the right thing to do. It can make a big difference to the people you know and meet. Try this activity to keep track of your helpfulness all month. See how being helpful really adds up.

What You Need:

- weekly or monthly calendar
- stickers (use stars, hearts, or whatever you like)
- notebook
- pencil or pen

What You Do:

1. Try to be helpful whenever you can. At the end of each day, think about how you helped people. Put a sticker on your calendar for each day you were helpful.

2. Use your notebook to write about how you helped others. Write about how it made you feel too.

3. At the end of the week, count how many stickers you put on your calendar.

4. After one month, look at your calendar. Count the stickers. How many times were you helpful?

5. Look carefully at the whole month. Do you see any patterns? Were you more helpful on weekends or during the week? Were you more helpful the first week or the last week? Write what you learned in your notebook. Then think of new ways you can help people!

Glossary

chore (CHOR)—a job that must be done regularly

community (kuh-MYOO-nuh-tee)—a group of people who live in the same area

confidence (KON-fuh-duhns)—a feeling that you can do well

donate (DOH-nayt)—to give something as a gift

litter (LIT-ur)—garbage that is scattered around carelessly

recycle (ree-SYE-kuhl)—to make used items into new products; people can recycle items such as rubber, glass, plastic, and aluminum

respect (ri-SPEKT)—to believe in the quality and worth of others and yourself

superpower (soo-pur-POW-ur)—an important skill that can affect yourself and others in a big way

volunteer (vol-uhn-TIHR)—to offer to do something without pay

Read More

Bell, Samantha. *12 Stories About Helping Seniors.* Mankato, MN: 12-Story Library, 2020.

Jacobson, Bray. *I Listen!* Buffalo, NY: Gareth Stevens Publishing, 2024.

VanVoorst, Jenny Fretland. *I Am Helpful.* Minneapolis: Bellwether Media, Inc.: 2019.

Internet Sites

DK FindOut!: Keeping Healthy
dkfindout.com/uk/human-body/keeping-healthy/

PBS Kids Talk About: Kindness!
pbs.org/video/pbs-kids-talk-about-kindness-tpcec6/

Sesame Workshop: Helping Others
sesameworkshop.org/resources/helping-others/

Index

chores, 4, 10, 11, 13
community, 6
confidence, 6

eating healthy, 18

kindness, 6, 14

litter, 16

recess, 14
recycling, 16

schoolwork, 15
sharing, 15
staying active, 18
stress, 18

teammates, 4
thoughtfulness, 6, 14

volunteering, 9

About the Author

Mari Schuh's love of reading began with cereal boxes at the kitchen table. Today she is the author of hundreds of nonfiction books for beginning readers. Mari lives in the Midwest with her husband and their sassy house rabbit. Learn more about her at marischuh.com.

158.3 S   FLO
Schuh, Mari C.,
Helpfulness is a superpower /

FLORES
07/24

DISCARD